LIFE'S TOUGHEST QUESTIONS
Erwin Raphael McManus

Small-Group Experience written by
Jason Jaggard

Life's Toughest Questions
Small-Group Study Guide
Published by LifeWay Christian Resources
©2010 Erwin McManus

All rights reserved. No part of this work may be reproduced, stored in a retrieval system, or transmitted in any form or by any means, electronic or mechanical, including photo-copying and recording, without express written permission of the publisher. Request for permission should be addressed to LifeWay Christian Resources, One LifeWay Plaza, Nashville, TN 37234-0175.

ISBN: 978-1-4158-6706-8
Item 005189414

Dewey Decimal Classification: 248.84
Subject Heading: CHRISTIAN LIFE \ DECISION MAKING \ CRITICAL THINKING

Unless otherwise marked, Scripture quotations are taken from the Holman Christian Standard Bible®, copyright © 1999, 2000, 2002, 2003 by Holman Bible Publishers. Used by permission. Scriptures marked NIV are from the Holy Bible, New International Version, copyright © 1973, 1978, 1984 by International Bible Society. Scriptures marked NCV are from the New Century Version. Copyright © 1987, 1988, 1991 by Thomas Nelson, Inc. Used by permission. All rights reserved. Scriptures marked NASB are taken from the New American Standard Bible®, Copyright © 1960, 1962, 1963, 1968, 1971, 1972, 1973, 1975, 1977, 1995 by The Lockman Foundation. Used by permission. (*www.lockman.org*)

To order additional copies of this resource, order online at *www.lifeway.com;* write LifeWay Small Groups; One LifeWay Plaza; Nashville, TN 37234-0175; fax order to (615) 251-5933; or call toll-free (800) 458-2772.

Printed in the United States of America

Leadership and Adult Publishing
LifeWay Church Resources
One LifeWay Plaza
Nashville, TN 37234-0175

CONTENTS

Behind the Curtain — 4

About This Study — 5

SESSION 1
Does God Care? — 6

SESSION 2
Is There a Hell? — 20

SESSION 3
What About Sex? — 36

SESSION 4
Is Jesus the Only Way? — 50

SESSION 5
Is Faith Nonsense? — 66

SESSION 6
Is God in Your Future? — 82

Group Directory — 96

BEHIND THE CURTAIN

⁷ Ask and it will be given to you; seek and you will find; knock and the door will be opened to you. ⁸ For everyone who asks receives; he who seeks finds; and to him who knocks, the door will be opened. – Matthew 7:7-8 (NIV)

Life is full of questions, but when it comes to the deep, significant questions that stir our souls, it's more demanding to find the answers that satisfy our hearts.

In preparation for this series, people from around the world were invited to submit the toughest questions facing them today. And in response, Erwin uses the Scriptures to lead us to grapple with some of the most meaningful and difficult issues in life.

The questions cover a broad range of issues but all bring us back to the undeniable truth that we are loved without condition by the One who shouldn't love us at all. We are the very objects of His love. He created us in His image and likeness and He treasures us ... deeply.

ABOUT THIS STUDY

Welcome to *Life's Toughest Questions*—a small-group Bible study from the *Platform* series. In this small-group experience, best-selling author and storyteller Erwin McManus leads us as we grapple with some of the most meaningful and difficult issues in life.

Here are the elements you'll be encountering during this small-group experience:

- **Warm-Up** – a time for sharing stories
- **Video Set-Up** – establishes context for your small-group time
- **Viewer Guide** – integral points from the video message to enhance discussion
- **Biblical Background** – biblical insight for greater understanding
- **Scripture** – all primary Scriptures are printed in the study guide
- **Small-Group Questions** – application, self-revelation, interpretation, or observation (discovery Bible study method builds community, invites God, and generates transformational discussion)
- **Journal** – contributes to personal devotional time
- **You're Up** – a challenge for group members to practice what they have learned
- **Leader Notes** - in colored text at the beginning of each section

Let your transformation begin!

SESSION 1

Does God Care?

Asking the question, "Does God exist?" takes us into apologetic defenses, arguments, and the highest heights of philosophical reasoning. Many would say it is the most important question in the world. Yet could there be a question that is even more important?

The question, "Does God care?" has divided friends and family. The most brilliant men and women have debated it for thousands of years. It cuts to the heart of our view of the world in which we live. It shapes our view of ourselves. Like politics and education, it is a question nearly everyone has an opinion about and an opinion nearly every person cares about.

WARM UP

Try not to spend too much time here, but let everyone answer the warm-up questions. Getting group members involved early helps create the best small-group environment.

List five fictional characters—from movies, books, fairy tales, holidays. If these characters existed, how much would it affect your life on a day-to-day basis? How much would it affect your life when suffering came?

VIDEO SET UP

The information below sets up the video. It can be read aloud to the group, read by group members ahead of time, or group members can read the information silently while the facilitator sets up the video.

For the most part, whether or not Santa, Indiana Jones, or Uncle Scrooge exist doesn't affect our lives. The idea of Santa may impact our shopping habits once a year. Indiana Jones would have died several decades ago. And an old miser living in the 19th century doesn't really influence our Facebook® pages, gas prices, or relationships.

Some people feel the same way about God. They agree that maybe He does exist, but they don't necessarily believe His existence impacts them—much less that He cares about them.

Could this be the great dilemma of our souls? Not asking the intellectual question of whether or not God exists but asking the more profound question of whether or not He actually cares?

How might the realization that God cares change our lives and even heal our souls?

Take a moment to read the Scripture passages on page 12 before watching "Does God Care?" (16:30). Then discuss the two questions designed as follow-up to the video on the Viewer Guide page.

SHOW VIDEO NOW.

VIEWER GUIDE

Included are two questions designed as follow-up to "Does God Care?" This time is set aside for discussion within the group about what they heard, how it affected them, and possible applications. These questions may be only a beginning. Feel free to begin the conversation by asking what thoughts, insights, or stories had the most impact on group members.

> **"It's one thing to come to know that God exists. It's another thing when you come to know that He cares."**

1. Jesus doesn't always take away our pain—sometimes He leaves us in our loss. According to Erwin's message, what can we know to be true about God even in those times?

2. What is God's primary motivation? What evidence do we have of that? *love*

BIBLICAL BACKGROUND

With music there is usually a story behind the song that helps listeners appreciate the heart and soul behind both the music and the lyrics. Scripture is no different. Below you'll find a brief story behind this week's Scripture intended to provide additional understanding and insight.

In the story of Lazarus, Jesus approaches the home of His deceased friend. In Jewish tradition, when someone died or some other tragedy occurred, people would often hire mourners to come and cry in order to create a sense of sorrow. The tears were real but the sorrow wasn't.

This is what made Jesus' tears so unique. When the onlookers expressed "See how He loved him!" (John 11:36) they were marveling about how Jesus' weeping wasn't just another paid performance; it was an honest expression.

The passage in Isaiah is prophetic literature. This type of literature has two general characteristics. The first is that it describes the future—probably the most common definition of "prophet." The second is that it calls people to create a better future. Martin Luther King, Jr. and Gandhi might be considered by some as prophets in this sense. All prophets in the Scriptures were both—they described the future as well as called the people of Israel to create a better future.

SCRIPTURE

Jesus wept. – John 11:35 (NIV)

¹⁹ **Everything God made is waiting with excitement for God to show his children's glory completely. ...** ²¹ **everything God made would be set free from ruin to have the freedom and glory that belong to God's children.** – Romans 8:19,21 (NCV)

"Pain helps us know something is broken."

¹ **Then I saw a new heaven and a new earth, ...** ³ **And I heard a loud voice from the throne saying, "Now the dwelling of God is with men, and he will live with them. They will be his people, and God himself will be with them and be their God.** ⁴ **He will wipe every tear from their eyes. There will be no more death or mourning or crying or pain, ...** ⁵ **I [God] am making everything new!"** – Revelation 21:1,3-5 (NIV)

If anyone is in Christ, he is a new creation; the old has gone, the new has come! – 2 Corinthians 5:17 (NIV)

He was wounded for the wrong we did;
   he was crushed for the evil we did.
The punishment, which made us well, was given to him,
   and we are healed because of his wounds.
– Isaiah 53:5 (NCV)

God has always been motivated by love.

SMALL-GROUP QUESTIONS

Over the next few pages you'll find discussion questions, material that may be used as additional discussion points, and a journal exercise for group members to complete away from the group.

> "How many times in our lives have we been in a moment and we've cried out to God and it just seemed as if the universe was silent?"

1. Have you ever felt like God wasn't there when you needed Him? Or been with someone who searched for God in a time of pain and suffering but couldn't seem to find Him? Share an example.

2. How do you usually interact with God in times like you just shared?

> **"The first reason we suffer is it's self-inflicted, and we need to take responsibility for it. … There's enough food on this planet to feed every hungry person on this earth. We just don't want to."**

3. What do you think it is about the human condition that makes it so easy to blame God for suffering instead of taking responsibility for the way we treat other people?

4. What are some excuses people give for not stepping up to help alleviate suffering in the world?

5. How do you think the consequences of our own decisions and influences (or lack of influence) can be reconciled with the fact that God is sovereign?

Global warming. Cancer. Hurricanes. Disease. We didn't choose these things, but Scripture teaches that as humans disconnected from God, the world God originally created as good began to experience these consequences. Insurance agencies call them "acts of God." They are natural consequences of living in a fallen world.

6. Is it possible that God could be both immanent (near, indwelling) and eminent (high, unreachable)? Explain.

7. What is God's response when things happen to us that are outside of our control?

CHAOS THEORY

This theory, made famous by Ian Malcolm in the film *Jurassic Park* (1993), is a combination of physics, mathematics, and philosophy to explain the unpredictability of complex systems. The famed "butterfly effect" (for instance, the wings of a butterfly flapping in Brazil causing a hurricane in the Gulf of Mexico) shows the theoretical interconnectedness of every particle of matter in the universe.

Whether or not it's true that every action we take is connected to a series of actions and reactions of every other particle of matter in the universe, we know that the world is more complicated than we realize. It is more of a mystery than we realize. Yet our actions, and the actions of people who have lived over the course of human history, have had effects—both positive and negative—in ways that we will never fully understand.

> "[God] not only embraces our pain but He takes it upon Himself. And all the suffering, all the evil, all the wickedness, all the wounding He bore on Himself so that through His wounds all of us might be healed."

8. C. S. Lewis refers to this sacrifice, healing, and reconciliation as a "deeper magic." Reread the Scriptures on page 12 and discuss the ways God heals us.

9. Do you think God is willing to step into your pain with you? Why or why not?

JOURNAL

This journaling opportunity is designed for group members to utilize at another time. They may choose to answer the question in the space provided or they may prefer to use the space and time to take a deep question or concern to God.

> **"Our world is in disarray because our hearts are in disarray. And God is the One who's proactively intervening to diminish the destructive effect of our actions and to act with compassion and love so that we might find His healing in the midst of our suffering."**

How does knowing and understanding more of the backstory of who God is, why He created us, and how He passionately loves us change your life and even heal your soul?

YOU'RE UP

As you think about connecting with God in your pain and joining with Him to alleviate the pain of others in the world, make time to do the following:

- Examine instances when you have had a tendency to incorrectly place blame for the suffering in the world or your life. Ask God to show you His truth.

- Ask God to use this week's Scripture passages to remind you of how much He cares.

- Spend some time thinking about obstacles you might be putting up between you and God that get in the way of you experiencing His compassion and love.

- Think of some ways you can take more initiative in alleviating the suffering of others.

Next week we will look at the question, "Is there a hell?" To prepare, take a minute to read Matthew 23:13-15,27-37; Revelation 3:20; Malachi 4:1-3; and Jude 22-23.

SESSION 2

Is There a Hell?

Hell. Possibly the most gruesome concept in the human imagination. Definitely the most controversial in the world of religion. It gets at the roots of some of our deepest insecurities: being wrong, rejected, oppressed, isolated, and punished. Few topics seem to make essentially good people become so arrogant and venomous. From offensive slogans like "Turn or Burn" to people holding signs, —there is so much emotion, so many layers associated with this explosive conversation. The troubling question hasn't changed much over the course of centuries: How can a good, benevolent God send people to hell? Let's talk about it.

WARM UP

Try not to spend too much time here, but let everyone answer the warm-up questions. Getting group members involved early helps create the best small-group environment.

Have you ever been left out of something? Maybe it was a job you wanted, or a relationship. Maybe it was a team or even your own family. How did that feel?

VIDEO SET UP

The information below sets up the video. It can be read aloud to the group, read by group members ahead of time, or group members can read the information silently while the facilitator sets up the video.

How should we wrestle with the reality of hell? What do the Scriptures teach? What have we been taught?

Christians have at times been guilty of defending hell with too much passion. It's not that we are passionate about hell—quite the contrary. We are passionate about saving others from an eternity apart from God. Even so, sometimes we become more obsessed with being right and imparting facts than with relationship and compassion. In this sense it seems that hell and compassion cannot coexist and that's where questions about the existence of hell begin to emerge.

Let's begin by killing the drama—hell is an actual place and there are and will be those who choose not to follow Christ. And because God honors our choices, He not only allows us to choose separation from Him but also grieves that decision.

Could it be that Jesus is trying to tell us about love? About life? What happens when you believe in a God who is committed to beauty, compassion, and also free choice?

Take a moment to read the Scripture passages on pages 26-27 before watching "Is There a Hell?" (18:30). Then discuss the two questions designed as follow-up to the video on the Viewer Guide page.

SHOW VIDEO NOW.

VIEWER GUIDE

Included are two questions designed as follow-up to "Is There a Hell?" This time is set aside for discussion within the group about what they heard, how it affected them, and possible applications. These questions may be only a beginning. Feel free to begin the conversation by asking what thoughts, insights, or stories had the most impact on group members.

1. Based on Erwin's message, who is most in danger of the reality of hell? Explain.

2. Does this way of thinking differ from what you have traditionally thought or been taught about hell? In what ways?

BIBLICAL BACKGROUND

With music there is usually a story behind the song that helps listeners appreciate the heart and soul behind both the music and the lyrics. Scripture is no different. Below you'll find a brief story behind this week's Scripture intended to provide additional understanding and insight.

The concept of hell has a strange evolution in the Scriptures. In Hebrew Scripture there was no word for "hell." There was *sheol* which was more literally "the grave." As Jerusalem was built, there was a valley outside the city called Gehenna. In history this was where followers of Baal would make sacrifices, sometimes burning their own children alive.

During the times of Jesus, Gehenna had become a giant garbage site where all the corpses, trash, and waste were dumped. The imagery is of things burning, ash, dogs running about eating the dead and the destroyed.

Gehenna was also where the outcasts were sent. Those who were dangerous, mentally unstable, crippled, lame, and any others who were deemed "unclean" could be found in this dreadful place. Consequently, the name *Gehenna* became a metaphor for life outside the city, life without God.

SCRIPTURE

---

¹³ How terrible for you, teachers of the law and Pharisees! You are hypocrites! You close the door for people to enter the kingdom of heaven. You yourselves don't enter, and you stop others who are trying to enter. ... ¹⁵ How terrible for you, teachers of the law and Pharisees! You are hypocrites! You travel across land and sea to find one person who will change to your ways. When you find that person, you make him more fit for hell than you are. – Matthew 23:13,15 (NCV)

Jerusalem, Jerusalem! You kill the prophets and stone to death those who are sent to you. Many times I wanted to gather your people as a hen gathers her chicks under her wings, but <u>you did not let me.</u> – Matthew 23:37 (NCV)

Behold, I stand at the door and knock; if anyone hears My voice and opens the door, I will come in to him and will dine with him, and he with Me. – Revelation 3:20 (NASB)

God will never force you to love Him. His driving theme is LOVE - not about geography but relationships

¹ "There is a day coming that will burn like a hot furnace, and all the proud and evil people will be like straw. On that day they will be completely burned up so that not a root or branch will be left," says the Lord All-Powerful. ² "But for you who honor me, goodness will shine on you like the sun, with healing in its rays. You will jump around, like well-fed calves. ³ Then you will crush the wicked like ashes under your feet on the day I will do this," says the Lord All-Powerful. – Malachi 4:1-3 (NCV)

²² Show mercy to some people who have doubts. ²³ Take others out of the fire, and save them. Show mercy mixed with fear to others, hating even their clothes which are dirty from sin. – Jude 22-23 (NCV)

Jesus talked of Hell to those who knew of Hell (check this) people @ center of religion" "pretenders" "hypocrites"

SMALL-GROUP QUESTIONS

Over the next few pages you'll find discussion questions, material that may be used as additional discussion points, and a journal exercise for group members to complete away from the group.

1. How would you describe a relationship where one person tries to force the other to love him or her?

WHEN LOVE FAILS

I think the first time we fall in love paradoxically is the best and worst experience of our lives. For me (Jason), the first time I fell in love I had no idea what I was doing. I remember telling my poor, unsuspecting girlfriend those three sacred words: "I love you." It meant a lot to her. She gazed into my eyes, smiled, and said, "I like you, too."

Six months later you could see the flames of our failing relationship for miles. Crash and burn. As she tried to break up with me I tried to convince her that we were *so* in love. It was pathetic (and maybe more than a little creepy). I can see that now. And so I experienced for the first time the pain of realizing people are free to make their own choices; that you can never demand love, you can only give it. And to try and force it is creepy at best, and wrong at worst.

> **"Hell exists not because God does not choose us, but because we do not choose Him. ... Hell is the place where you say, 'No, I don't want your love.'"**

2. Have you ever rejected someone or something and later realized it was a mistake? Explain.

REEL STORIES

Forrest Gump (1994) tells the story of a unique man, the amazing life he lived, and the people he interacted with along the way. Through his journey he falls in love with Jenny—a young woman who is on a journey of her own. We see Jenny struggle with love— from being abused as a child to learning how to receive the pure love of an unlikely man. Forrest tells Jenny: "I may not be a smart man, but I do know what love is." His is a love from which Jenny runs for the better part of her life. We see through her pain and struggles what a life running from love can look like.

In the end Jenny chooses to embrace the love that has always been there. A tragic ending leads us to mixed emotions of happiness for Jenny and Forrest as well as a sense of regret. Life doesn't have to be lived without love.

"Hell exists because God refuses to override your will."

3. What do you think it says about God that He honors our choices?

4. What would we lose if God didn't honor our choices but instead chose to "override" our will?

> **"We want to have the freedom to choose but we don't want to have to embrace the responsibility for our choices."**

God will stop the violence.
Mal 4:1-3

5. What responsibilities come with exercising our freedom to choose?

6. What are the benefits of having this freedom? The drawbacks? Explain.

"We should all have the smell of smoke on our clothes."

7. Discuss the ways we can identify and engage those who are searching for or running from the love of God.

8. Jude 22-23 directs us to show mercy to some and mercy mixed with fear to others. What do you think are the differences and how do you think we're to know?

JOURNAL

This journaling opportunity is designed for group members to utilize at another time. They may choose to answer the question in the space provided or they may prefer to use the space and time to take a deep question or concern to God.

What is your attitude toward people who—according to the religious—are going to hell? What is your attitude toward the religious who—according to Jesus—are in more danger of hell than we think? What things can you do to move more toward God and, as you do, move more toward people who are searching for God?

YOU'RE UP

As you wrestle with the reality of hell and what it says about God and humanity, consider doing the following:

- Ask God to give you a heart of compassion for those who are suffering without Him.

- Reflect on the Scriptures and ask God to show you what your response should be to a world searching for Him.

- Enjoy the possibility of being able to partner with God to serve people searching for Him, to snatch some from the fire, and to have the smell of smoke on your clothes.

Next week we will look at the question, "What about sex?" To prepare, take a few minutes to read 1 Corinthians 3:16-17; 6:9-20; Romans 1:21-32; and Psalm 37:4.

SESSION 3

What About Sex?

Earlier we looked at whether or not God cares about us and explored the beautiful possibility of a God who stepped into history to declare that He *does* care about humanity—our hurts and pains and struggles. Yet sometimes we don't want people to care. As good as it feels for someone to care when we're suffering, caring can become ... well ... invasive. Parents *care* about our grades. Bosses *care* about our work ethic. And while it's good that God cares about our suffering, things get a little tricky when we discover that He also cares about our sexuality. He cares about intimacy, when we share our hearts, and when we become one. Our sexuality and intimacy are a big deal.

WARM UP

Try not to spend too much time here, but let everyone answer the warm-up question. Getting group members involved early helps create the best small-group environment.

Has there ever been a time when someone cared about a part of your life that you had not really made available to others? If so, describe why you felt resistant to their care and concern.

VIDEO SET UP

The information below sets up the video. It can be read aloud to the group, read by group members ahead of time, or group members can read the information silently while the facilitator sets up the video.

In what Erwin describes as his "least PC talk ever," we begin to explore a sexuality that is designed and influenced by God.

This can become a painful journey mired by self-righteousness, judgmentalism, and hypocrisy. From pastors moralizing from the pulpit while hiding their own secret sins, to people screaming awful slogans at the funerals of men and women who died from AIDS, the conversation about sex and homosexuality can quickly be hijacked by fear and anxiety.

What is at the core of this conversation? Erwin wrestles with these questions: *Does God care about how we treat each other? Does how we treat each other reveal what we value in life? Does how we treat each other apply to our sexuality and how we define love?*

While there are no easy answers to these questions, there are answers. These questions and answers lead us to have the highest possible view of humanity and how human beings were meant to treat each other.

Take a moment to read the Scripture passages on page 42 before watching "What About Sex?" (21:00). Then discuss the two questions designed as follow-up to the video on the Viewer Guide page

SHOW VIDEO NOW.

VIEWER GUIDE

Included are two questions designed as follow-up to "What About Sex?" This time is set aside for discussion within the group about what they heard, how it affected them, and possible applications. These questions may be only a beginning. Feel free to begin the conversation by asking what thoughts, insights, or stories had the most impact on group members.

1. Why might somebody not want God to care about his or her sexuality?

2. What could be lost by advocating this view?

BIBLICAL BACKGROUND

With music there is usually a story behind the song that helps listeners appreciate the heart and soul behind both the music and the lyrics. Scripture is no different. Below you'll find a brief story behind this week's Scripture intended to provide additional understanding and insight.

Erwin explores two passages, both written by Paul, an early leader of Christianity. One passage was written to a group of people in the ancient city of Corinth. The other to people in the ancient city of Rome. Both were cities of influence in the world at the time. The city of Corinth was known for its promiscuity and cultural advocacy for casual sex as a means of connecting to God.

The city of Rome was the cultural center. Paul's letter to the people in Rome takes a 50,000 foot perspective on who God is, who we are created to be, and how we tend to stray from that human ideal—not by means of design but by means of choice.

Both Corinthians and Romans were promoters of boundless sexual indulgence, and both were suffering from the pain such indulgences create. The people needed communities that helped shape a new picture of how healthy relationships can flourish and the kind of beautiful life those relationships can create. These two particular letters were written to help make that kind of community thrive in a world searching for genuine love and healthy relationships.

— Our relat to God affects our relat. w/ each other.

SCRIPTURE — *speaking to believers*

Corinth — sexual prostitutes — sex w/ them to grow closer to God.

¹⁶ **Don't you know that you are God's temple and that God's Spirit lives in you?** ¹⁷ **If anyone destroys God's temple, God will destroy that person, because God's temple is holy and you are that temple.** – 1 Corinthians 3:16-17 (NCV)

¹³ **The body** *(to believers in Corinth)* **is not for sexual sin but for the Lord, and the Lord is for the body. …** ¹⁵ **Surely you know that your bodies are parts of Christ himself. So I must never take the parts of Christ and join them to a prostitute! …** ¹⁷ **But the one who joins with the Lord is one spirit with the Lord.** ¹⁸ **So run away from sexual sin. Every other sin people do is outside their bodies, but those who sin sexually sin against their own bodies. …** ¹⁹ **Your body is a temple for the Holy Spirit who is in you. …** ²⁰ **So honor God with your bodies.**
– 1 Corinthians 6:13,15,17-20 (NCV)

²⁴ **Because they did these things, God left them and let them go their sinful way, … they became full of sexual sin, using their bodies wrongly with each other.** ²⁵ **They traded the truth of God for a lie. …** ²⁶ **Women stopped having natural sex and started having sex with other women.** ²⁷ **Men did shameful things with other men, and in their bodies they received the punishment for those wrongs.** – Romans 1:24-27 (NCV)

making choices against what God wants for us destroys our souls.

[Handwritten notes at top: "our relat to unbelieving world → to show them uncondit love / God has a higher value for human beings than we do!"]

SMALL-GROUP QUESTIONS

Over the next few pages you'll find discussion questions, material that may be used as additional discussion points, and a journal exercise for group members to complete away from the group.

> "For too long it's been so easy for Christians to be judgmental and arrogant to people without God. ... when the reality is we have one relationship to an unbelieving world—and that's just to love them. But to us on the inside, the message is more stark."

1. What evidence do you see that Christians have fallen into the trap of challenging the world and excusing themselves rather than loving the world and challenging themselves?

2. How do you think this has shaped the current conversation on sexuality between the church and the broader society?

REEL STORIES

The film *Crash* (2004) deals with the stereotypes that exist when different people with different viewpoints collide. In the film, Sandra Bullock's character is written as racist and judgmental, especially toward her housekeeper. As the story progresses, situations occur that help each character see the other in a new way—a way that more resembles how they see themselves. Sandra's character is involved in an accident after which she has to rely on her housekeeper to take care of her. Going through that vulnerable experience opened her heart to the humanity of both of them and finally, love was able to take hold. The film explores how love has a tendency to bridge the gap between even the most seemingly different people. It is a parable that challenges us to love our neighbors as ourselves, no matter where they're coming from.

"What you do to your body matters to God, because you are the most valuable creation of God. ... You are created for intimacy with God and so everything you're intimate with you drag God into it."

3. How might this notion that you are God's most valuable creation and 1 Corinthians 6:13,15 affect the relationships in your life?

4. In what ways might this reality of who you are change how you treat yourself, your body in intimate relationships?

When we stop thinking right about God we stop thinking right about each other.

> "We live in a culture that's so terrified of intimacy and so longs for intimacy. The very thing you need most you're probably most afraid of."

5. How has our culture distorted the sanctity and purity of sexuality? In what ways do you think this has contributed to the fear Erwin references?

> "It is right to love people of the opposite sex *and* the same sex. We keep confusing erotic desires with genuine love."

6. How do you think this confusion applies to both homosexuality and heterosexuality?

As you fall in & w/ God, He changes us from the inside. The driving force of our life is love. It changes how

7. How would you define, in your own words, a biblical view of love? (See 1 Corinthians 13 to get started.)

8. What implications might this view of love have on your sexuality?

"Delight yourself in the Lord and he will give you the desires of your heart." – Psalm 37:4 (NIV)

9. In what ways could you begin trusting God with the way you love others? How might the act of trusting God change the way you treat sex in intimate relationships?

we relate to each other.

JOURNAL

This journaling opportunity is designed for group members to utilize at another time. They may choose to answer the question in the space provided or they may prefer to use the space and time to take a deep question or concern to God.

How is your sexuality shaping your relationships? In what ways could you begin aligning those relationships to reflect God's design for how we should treat each other with genuine love?

YOU'RE UP

While you consider God's role and will in your sexuality, consider these first steps:

- Ask God to help you see yourself as more than just a sexual being.

- Reflect on the Scriptures and ask God to speak to you in response to your own struggles with sexuality and relationships.

- Refuse to believe the lie that you were born with a certain sexual orientation. Embrace the reality of your own sexual development and where that development needs to go in the future.

- Begin to align your relationships to reflect God's design for love.

Next week we will look at the question, "Is Jesus the only way?" To prepare, take a minute to read Deuteronomy 30:11-20; 1 John 4:7-12; and John 15:9-15.

SESSION 4

Is Jesus the Only Way?

How do we best connect to God? There are so many competing worldviews, beliefs, and religions. There have been so many wars over who's right and who's wrong. Crusades. Caste Systems. Terrorism. All waged by people in a seemingly endless game of "My god can beat up your god." It seems so destructive. It *is* so destructive. And buried underneath the wars and conflicts is this Middle Eastern rabbi who only led in a public way for three short years. Did Jesus really teach that He was the only way to God? Wouldn't a loving God accept all paths, justify all beliefs? During this small-group time we're going to explore the truths of the gospel and how Jesus is the only way.

WARM UP

Try not to spend too much time here, but let everyone answer the warm-up question. Getting group members involved early helps create the best small-group environment.

At one time or another we've all felt rejected. Maybe it was a break-up or a job you didn't get. Maybe somebody didn't come to your party, you didn't get picked for the team, or someone talked about you behind your back. Share your story and spend some time exploring why rejection is so traumatic.

VIDEO SET UP

The information below sets up the video. It can be read aloud to the group, read by group members ahead of time, or group members can read the information silently while the facilitator sets up the video.

Rejection is one of the most painful of all human experiences. So what message is being sent when we hear that "God will reject you unless you accept His Son"?

Saying Jesus is the only way comes across as a slap in the face to every Buddhist, Muslim, Jew, and Hindu. It becomes a conversation that has nothing to do with love and everything to do with who's right and who's wrong.

Is it possible that God is not rejecting us but is in fact pursuing us? Is it possible that it isn't God rejecting humanity but humanity rejecting God? Could the conversation be about where we find life and not about who is right? In the video you're about to watch, Erwin explores the possibility of seeing the reality of the gospel not as rejection, but as God's pursuit of us.

Take a moment to read the Scripture passages on pages 56-57 before watching "Is Jesus the Only Way?" (19:43). Then discuss the two questions designed as follow-up to the video on the Viewer Guide page.

SHOW VIDEO NOW.

VIEWER GUIDE

Included are two questions designed as follow-up to "Is Jesus the Only Way?" This time is set aside for discussion within the group about what they heard, how it affected them, and possible applications. These questions may be only a beginning. Feel free to begin the conversation by asking what thoughts, insights, or stories had the most impact on group members.

1. What choice is laid out in the Deuteronomy passage Erwin shares in his message? Have you ever made a choice that literally saved your life? Explain.

2. What was the most powerful thing you learned from Erwin's message about the heart and desire of God for people?

BIBLICAL BACKGROUND

With music there is usually a story behind the song that helps listeners appreciate the heart and soul behind both the music and the lyrics. Scripture is no different. Below you'll find a brief story behind this week's Scripture intended to provide additional understanding and insight.

The passage in Deuteronomy 30 is part of God's interaction with the people of Israel. Passages of Scripture like these can often be looked at as a list of rules or a series of hoops to jump through in order to please God. But the laws and commands of the Old Testament aren't so much about arbitrary hoops as they are paths that lead to the kind of life God wanted for the Israelites then and for us today. In short, there is a way to do life in order to maximize fulfillment and a way to do life destructively.

The other two passages Erwin looks at are written by John. John was close to Jesus. In those days, many rabbis would have a particular disciple who was protected more closely by the rabbi, had a special nickname, and was around 13 or 14 years old. Many scholars believe John was that disciple for Jesus. This could explain why he lived to a later date than any of the other disciples and why—on the cross—Jesus made sure His mother and John were connected.

Jesus called John "the disciple Jesus loved." To John, being loved by Jesus was a central part of his identity—who he was as a human being.

God says "I'm right here!"

SCRIPTURE

What God wants for us!

¹¹ What I am commanding you today is not too difficult for you. ...

¹⁵ See, I set before you today life and prosperity, death and destruction. ¹⁶ For I command you today to love the LORD your God, to walk in his ways, and to keep his commands, decrees and laws; then you will live and increase, and the LORD your God will bless you in the land you are entering to possess.

¹⁷ But if your heart turns away and you are not obedient, and if you are drawn away to bow down to other gods and worship them, ¹⁸ I declare to you this day that you will certainly be destroyed. ...

¹⁹ This day I call heaven and earth as witnesses against you that I have set before you life and death, blessings and curses. (Now choose life,) so that you and your children may live ²⁰ and that you may love the LORD your God, listen to his voice, and hold fast to him. (For the LORD is your life,) and he will give you many years in the land he swore to give to your fathers, Abraham, Isaac and Jacob. – Deuteronomy 30:11,15-20 (NIV)

God's telling us that He is life itself. God is the Source of life. Jesus is the only one who cares about you & came for you! There is no other God who loves you & longs to heal you from your brokenness.

When you choose God, love expands. Love is not a limited commodity

> ⁷ Dear friends, let us love one another, for love comes from God. Everyone who loves has been born of God and knows God. ⁸ Whoever does not love does not know God, because God is love. ⁹ This is how God showed his love among us: He sent his one and only Son into the world that we might live through him. ¹⁰ This is love: not that we loved God, but that he loved us and sent his Son as an atoning sacrifice for our sins. ¹¹ Dear friends, since God so loved us, we also ought to love one another. ¹² No one has ever seen God; but if we love one another, God lives in us and his love is made complete in us.
> – 1 John 4:7-12 (NIV)

> ⁹ As the Father has loved me, so have I loved you. Now remain in my love. ¹⁰ If you obey my commands, you will remain in my love, just as I have obeyed my Father's commands and remain in his love. ¹¹ I have told you this so that my joy may be in you and that <u>your joy may be complete</u>. ¹² My command is this: Love each other as I have loved you. ¹³ Greater love has no one than this, that he lay down his life for his friends. ¹⁴ You are my friends if you do what I command. ¹⁵ I no longer call you servants, because a servant does not know his master's business. Instead, I have called you friends, for everything that I learned from my Father I have made known to you. – John 15:9-15 (NIV)

Jesus came to make you His friend.

Check every other world religion to see if they have a god that loves you & would sacrifice Himself for you!

Before

SMALL-GROUP QUESTIONS

Over the next few pages you'll find discussion questions, material that may be used as additional discussion points, and a journal exercise for group members to complete away from the group.

> "God creates you with the capacity to choose,
> the freedom to choose."

*Freedom exists so love can exist.
We are objects of God's love.*

1. Do you see choice as more liberating or burdensome?

REEL STORIES

In *Indiana Jones and the Last Crusade* (1989) there's the iconic scene where Indiana Jones has to guess from a room full of cups which cup Jesus drank from at the last supper. "Whoever drinks from this cup will live forever" the old knight protecting the room says. With his father dying from a gunshot wound, Jones desperately looks over all the cups and goblets. Some are adorned with beautiful jewels and made of gold.

Before Jones can make a choice, the villain in the film rushes past him and grabs the most elaborate goblet. He dips it in the water and drinks deeply from the cup. He then quickly ages and disintegrates until his bones are blown against the back of the cavern.

The ancient knight looks at Indiana and says three famous words: "He chose … poorly."

Indiana's task seemed like a test or an elaborate game. Too often we look at God in much the same way: like a cosmic gamer who's waiting to see what we will choose, only to punish us if we don't choose wisely.

> **"God isn't telling us He's going to kill us because we don't choose Him. He's telling us that He is life itself. So when we don't choose Him we choose death."**

2. How would you define "life"? What might be some choices that lead people toward life?

3. How would you define figurative "death"? What might be some choices that lead people toward death?

A PERSONAL BENT

A few years ago I (Jason) was in a relationship with a girl I had been dating for several years. We had gone through pre-engagement counseling, but I was afraid to commit to marriage. It was obvious to everyone else that she was in love with me, but for whatever reason I didn't feel the same.

The way I came to understand it later was that dating can be like buying a used car. You walk around, studying the car. You kick the tires. You take it for a test run. After two years, the girl I was dating got tired of being a test run. On a warm night in the middle of May she told me our relationship was over.

What might surprise you is how crushed I was. No, *devastated*. Her decision threw me into a tailspin that opened up parts of my heart I didn't even know I had. I began to have feelings I didn't know I was capable of having.

Two months later I asked her to marry me.

You see, I needed something painful to break my heart open so it could receive love. Sometimes heartbreak is the only way we learn how to love.

> **"There is no other god who loves you and passionately pursues you and longs to forgive you of your sin and heal you of your brokenness."**

4. Can you think of any other religion or worldview that has meaning and love searching for us rather than us searching for love and meaning? Explain.

5. How does this affect how you see God as revealed in Jesus as compared to other systems of belief?

God has always been FOR you!

> "When Jesus says He's the only way, He's not trying to establish some kind of arrogant, narcissistic exclusivity. He's telling you: I'm the One who loves you. I'm the One who's pursuing you. I'm the One who's willing to pay the price for your love, for your life. Choose Me and live."

6. Does the reality of the statement above impact how you see God? If so, in what ways?

7. Could it be more important for us to pursue life with God versus being right? How are these two thoughts different?

8. Think of the different areas of your life. In what ways might you need to be more alive?

JOURNAL

This journaling opportunity is designed for group members to utilize at another time. They may choose to answer the question in the space provided or they may prefer to use the space and time to take a deep question or concern to God.

What would it look like for you to begin receiving God's love in a deeper way?

What can you do to follow Jesus into living life more fully?

YOU'RE UP

To live more fully in the life Christ came to give you, consider acting on these things:

- Ask God to help you see Him as the path to truly living, rather than just avoiding hell, getting into heaven, or being right in an argument with those who disagree.

- Reflect on the Scriptures and ask God to reveal to you ways you can experience more life with Him, more compassion for others, more meaning, and more hope.

- In what ways can you help people see God as the source of life rather than just another choice among many? Ask God to open doors for you to carry these things out.

Next week we will look at the question, "Is faith nonsense?" To prepare, take a minute to read Genesis 3:6-12; Exodus 33:12-23; Isaiah 6:1-10; and 2 Corinthians 4.

SESSION 5

Is Faith Nonsense?

In the honest journey of searching for God, we inevitably run into the issue of faith. The question might be asked a million different ways, but at its core it sounds like this: *How do we believe in what we cannot see?* For some, this question is like a crack in a sidewalk that we just hop over. For others it feels like an ocean, impossible to swim. Faith can seem completely out of our grasp. How can something that seems so natural for others become available to us?

WARM UP

Try not to spend too much time here, but let everyone answer the warm-up question. Getting group members involved early helps create the best small-group environment.

What words would you use to describe faith?

unquestionable belief
evidence of things unseen
trust

VIDEO SET UP

The information below sets up the video. It can be read aloud to the group, read by group members ahead of time, or group members can read the information silently while the facilitator sets up the video.

Faith feels out of reach for some and foolish to others. It is not rational. It is not logical. Yet Scripture reveals its primal importance in connecting with God. The Bible says it is impossible to please God without faith. It talks about heroes of the past and how they moved forward to partner with God "in faith."

We get it: faith is important. Yet for many it is so hard to carry out. For most it is even harder to describe. Why is this so?

There has been much ink spilled in an attempt to "prove" how rational, reasonable, and easy it is to believe in God—to see the invisible and to experience the untouchable. Yet does all this arguing get us where we really want to go?

Today we address the question, "Is faith nonsense?" Erwin's answer? Absolutely, unequivocally, inarguably yes.

Take a moment to read the Scripture passages on pages 72-73 before watching "Is Faith Nonsense?" (25:37). Then discuss the two questions designed as follow-up to the video on the Viewer Guide page.

SHOW VIDEO NOW.

VIEWER GUIDE

Included are two questions designed as follow-up to "Is Faith Nonsense?" This time is set aside for discussion within the group about what they heard, how it affected them, and possible applications. These questions may be only a beginning. Feel free to begin the conversation by asking what thoughts, insights, or stories had the most impact on group members.

1. What do you think Erwin means when he describes faith as "nonsense"?

2. After listening to Erwin's message, how would you answer the question, "Why do we need faith?"

BIBLICAL BACKGROUND

With music there is usually a story behind the song that helps listeners appreciate the heart and soul behind both the music and the lyrics. Scripture is no different. Below you'll find a brief story behind this week's Scripture intended to provide additional understanding and insight.

Genesis tells the story of the spiritual origins of humanity. It not only tells the story of what happened then, but also of what's happening now. Genesis 3 specifically recounts the moment humanity separated itself from God in the garden of Eden.

Exodus and Isaiah flesh out the picture painted by the reality Genesis describes. God reveals Himself to both Moses and Isaiah in ways that illuminate the way people must interact with God in a post-Genesis world. Here, the lives of two great leaders intersect with God in a powerful way and the two men have surprisingly similar reactions.

Genesis helps us understand the problem; Exodus and Isaiah illustrate the consequences; and in 2 Corinthians the apostle Paul explains the solution.

SCRIPTURE

We can't see God in all His glory. God in all His glory would consume us in our condition.

[18] Then Moses said, "Now show me your glory." [19] And the LORD said, "I will cause all my goodness to pass in front of you, and I will proclaim my name, the LORD, in your presence. I will have mercy on whom I will have mercy, and I will have compassion on whom I will have compassion. [20] But," he said, "you cannot see my face, for no one may see me and live."

[21] Then the LORD said, "There is a place near me where you may stand on a rock. [22] When my glory passes by, I will put you in a cleft in the rock and cover you with my hand until I have passed by. [23] Then I will remove my hand and you will see my back; but my face must not be seen."

– Exodus 33:18-23 (NIV)

[3] And they were calling to one another:
> "Holy, holy, holy is the LORD Almighty;
> the whole earth is full of his glory."

[4] At the sound of their voices the doorposts and thresholds shook and the temple was filled with smoke.

[5] "Woe to me!" I cried. "I am ruined! For I am a man of unclean lips, and I live among a people of unclean lips, and my eyes have seen the King, the LORD Almighty."

There is empirical evidence of God in the world. We are defective in our capacity to see this reality.

"You can look at broken messed up people & see God in the cracks"

⁶ Then one of the seraphs flew to me with a live coal in his hand, which he had taken with tongs from the altar. ⁷ With it he touched my mouth and said, "See, this has touched your lips; your guilt is taken away and your sin atoned for."

⁸ Then I heard the voice of the Lord saying, "Whom shall I send? And who will go for us?"

And I said, "Here am I. Send me!" – Isaiah 6:3-8 (NIV)

One kingdom wants to keep us blind. The other wants to give us light. We who have this light are the evidence!

¹³ It is written: "I believed; therefore I have spoken." With that same spirit of faith we also believe and therefore speak, ¹⁴ because we know that the one who raised the Lord Jesus from the dead will also raise us with Jesus and present us with you in his presence. …

¹⁶ Therefore we do not lose heart. … ¹⁷ For our light and momentary troubles are achieving for us an eternal glory that far outweighs them all. ¹⁸ So we fix our eyes not on what is seen, but on what is unseen. For what is seen is temporary, but what is unseen is eternal.

– 2 Corinthians 4:13-14,16-18 (NIV)

God is constantly speaking into our lives. Our sin keeps us from being able to be completely in His presence. We're broken in our capacity to know God & even be aware of His presence.

Faith is the spiritual word for where you put your trust.

SMALL-GROUP QUESTIONS

Over the next few pages you'll find discussion questions, material that may be used as additional discussion points, and a journal exercise for group members to complete away from the group.

> "Have you ever had something in your gut tell you that something was going to happen but you don't know how you knew because none of your senses could validate it?"

1. How would you describe those things we can "sense" without the senses? How much decision-making do you attribute to this "sense"?

2. Are these senses to be trusted? Why or why not?

> "Faith is a non-sense. It is the language that w
> describe the fact that there is something [someo]
> there that exists, that our senses cannot perceive ade[

3. In light of this week's discussion so far, would you define faith differently than you did in the warm-up activity? If so, explain.

"Faith & reason aren't the same thing."

"someone/something that exists that our senses can't perceive"

"God isn't hiding from us – we hide from God & He's searching for us." (like Adam & Eve)

Glory of God – beautiful, majestic if our ♥ are toward God.
but terrifying if our ♥ are turned from God.

There's something broken in us.

"God makes His proof of Himself by changing us"

"He gives us the capacity to see the unseen."

"Thru transformation of our life He can be seen."

> "Why doesn't God just show up? ... It's not because He does not want to reveal Himself but because we cannot contain His presence."

When we get a sense of God's holiness, we tend to want to hide.

4. In Exodus 33:18 Moses asks God to show His glory. What does that mean to you?

5. Have you found yourself making similar requests of God? What was it you were really looking for in those instances?

REEL STORIES

In Disney's *Aladdin* (1992) there is an iconic scene where Aladdin asks Princess Jasmine to go with him on a carpet ride through the arid Arabian night. He holds out his hand, looks into her eyes, and says just four words: "Do you trust me?" At that point, Jasmine has no real reason—no rationality—for taking his hand. Carpets cannot fly. Yet something within her tells her that it's OK. Something in Aladdin's eyes convinces her that an adventure with this mysterious prince is better than going back into her bedroom. She goes in faith.

> **"God is making Himself known to all of us, but our capacity to perceive His existence is defective, which is where faith comes in."**

6. God tells us in Isaiah 42 that He will lead us down unknown paths. Does trusting God on an unknown path scare you or make you come alive? Explain.

7. Reread 2 Corinthians 4:18 on page 73. What adjustments do you need to make to focus on less of the visible and more of the eternal?

> **"God makes His proof of Himself by changing us."**

8. In what ways have you seen the proof of God in the lives of other people?

JOURNAL

This journaling opportunity is designed for group members to utilize at another time. They may choose to answer the question in the space provided or they may prefer to use the space and time to take a deep question or concern to God.

> "How does [God] make Himself known? ... By taking those who believe ... and giving us the capacity to see the unseen ... to hear that which is inaudible, and to know that which is unknowable ... and to be the proof of God."

How is God making Himself known in your life?

YOU'RE UP

To begin living out your faith fully, take these first steps:

- Ask God to help you sense Him in deeper and more profound ways. Ask Him to increase your faith. (Gulp!)

- Think of ways you can begin encouraging faith in others rather than trying to rationalize or argue about it.

- Reflect on the Scriptures and ask God to show you what areas of your life can grow to reflect who He is to a world searching for Him.

Next week we will look at the question, "Is God in your future?" To prepare, take a minute to read Daniel 2:45-46; 10:14; Jeremiah 29:11-14; 2 Kings 20:1-6; and Genesis 18:16-33.

Handwritten notes:
- Suzanne Miller - sing Tues
- John's sister - Glenna poor health
- John Bush - to Cleveland, OH abdominal surgery?

SESSION 6

Is God in Your Future?

"The future." It can seem so far away. The public discourse on the future is often limited to science fiction taking us "back to the future" or Christian books "left behind" on our bookshelves. After a while the future can seem so inaccessible. Often times it feels like the future is out there, waiting for us. Sometimes it feels like the future is breathing down our necks—a foreboding sense of doom. So whether the future seems far off or it's staring us right in the face, the questions remain: *What is our relationship with the future?* and *Who controls what the future will look like?*

WARM UP

Try not to spend too much time here, but let everyone answer the warm-up questions. Getting group members involved early helps create the best small-group environment.

What feelings come up for you when you think of the word *future*? Share how you're feeling about your future and why.

VIDEO SET UP

The information below sets up the video. It can be read aloud to the group, read by group members ahead of time, or group members can read the information silently while the facilitator sets up the video.

We don't create the future—God does. The past, present, and future are all fixed, with every act, thought, or feeling waiting to unfold in a predetermined way. Right?

Such a view can feel warm, cozy, and comforting. It safely removes us from any responsibility for how the world was, is, or is going to be. The burden of our lives is lifted off our shoulders. It's an attractive life with a great appeal to many.

Warmth. Rest. Comfort. Peace. These are great feelings. Then again, such feelings are also what you experience just before you freeze to death. And our wills are freezing.

Could there be a different way to look at the future? One that still gives us a sense of trust in God yet empowers us to act in the present to actually create the future in a real way? What do the Scriptures say about God and our future?

Take a moment to read the Scripture passages on page 88 before watching "Is God in Your Future?" (21:11). Then discuss the two questions designed as follow-up to the video on the Viewer Guide page.

SHOW VIDEO NOW.

VIEWER GUIDE

Included are two questions designed as follow-up to "Is God in Your Future?" This time is set aside for discussion within the group about what they heard, how it affected them, and possible applications. These questions may be only a beginning. Feel free to begin the conversation by asking what thoughts, insights, or stories had the most impact on group members.

1. Why might a person be more comfortable with the past than the future?

2. Based on what Erwin shares in his message, how would you interpret the phrase, "create the future"? How does that concept make you feel?

BIBLICAL BACKGROUND

With music there is usually a story behind the song that helps listeners appreciate the heart and soul behind both the music and the lyrics. Scripture is no different. Below you'll find a brief story behind this week's Scripture intended to provide additional understanding and insight.

For our conversation today, try to relax any presuppositions you may have and be open to interacting with the text in a new way. Enjoy being stretched and even amazed by the possibilities that these ancient stories suggest about us, God, and the future.

The ancient world was much more open in its competing views about the world. The Books of Daniel and Jeremiah involve people dialoguing about what God revealed to them regarding the future.

Luke's account in the Book of Acts illuminates the bizarre world of fortune tellers that we may dismiss today.

The Books of Genesis and Kings provide two examples of people who act and then God does the seemingly impossible: He reacts.

Such stories are often written off as trying to ascribe human characteristics to God. But could they in fact be the opposite? Could they be less about making God more human and more about making humanity more aware of its God-given potential to create the future with God?

II Kings 20 *Gen 18:16 - Abraham pleads w/ God for Sodom*

SCRIPTURE

The great God has shown the king what will take place in the future. The dream is true and the interpretation is trustworthy. – Daniel 2:45b (NIV)

Now I have come to explain to you what will happen to your people in the future, for the vision concerns a time yet to come. – Daniel 10:14 (NIV)

→ (thoughts, dreams, purpose ...)

¹¹ "For I know the plans I have for you," declares the Lord, "plans to prosper you and not to harm you, plans to give you hope and a future. ¹² Then you will call upon me and come and pray to me, and I will listen to you. ¹³ You will seek me and find me when you seek me with all your heart. ¹⁴ I will be found by you," declares the Lord. – Jeremiah 29:11-14 (NIV)

Go back and tell Hezekiah, the leader of my people, "This is what the Lord, the God of your father David, says: I have heard your prayer and seen your tears; I will heal you. On the third day from now you will go up to the temple of the Lord." – 2 Kings 20:5 (NIV)   *Hezekiah changes God's timetable?*

We will need to seek God — our part!
God is fully engaged in the future
& He wants us to be engaged in the future.
dynamic interplay betw God acting/engaging history & us engaging the future!

SMALL-GROUP QUESTIONS

Over the next few pages you'll find discussion questions, material that may be used as additional discussion points, and a journal exercise for group members to complete away from the group.

1. When you think of God, where is He usually—in the present, the future, or the past? Explain.

2. Why might it be important to think of God in terms of being in all three?

A VIEW OF THE FUTURE FROM THE FIRST GRADE

One of my favorite experiences when I (Jason) was in the first grade was going to assemblies. Sometimes it would be to watch a movie (*Chitty Chitty Bang Bang* fondly comes to mind), and other times it was for something educational or for an awards ceremony or a concert. What I remember most was that we—the first graders—sat up front. Then there were these giants—sixth graders. They were big. Some of them were smelly. They were intimidating. Every kid wanted to be in the sixth grade.

I remember talking with my friends about how far away the sixth grade felt. How it seemed like we would never be in the sixth grade. It was too far ahead to grasp.

Yesterday I got off the phone with my grandpa who has just turned 90. As we talked, I thought to myself, *90 seems so far away.* But now I know better.

The future is coming faster than we think. We can't stop it, but we *can* help create it.

- if we are godless, we don't feel the need to get permission to make (create) the future.
- violent seem to be most passionate about the future.
- Does God determine the future?
- * God is the composer + orchestrator of the future.
- God drives the future toward a conclusion.
- God explains the "what" but not usually the "how"

> **"God is absolutely engaged, aware, and shaping the future. God is the composer and orchestrator of the future."**

3. What do you think this says about how God interacts with history?

> **"There are moments in time where God unwraps this future and tells us a bit of what He's doing and where He's going ... He whispers into the souls of those who are willing to listen."**

4. Is this way of thinking different from how you have traditionally thought of God? In what ways?

"The future is less linear than it is liquid."

5. What would change in your life if you considered God's plans for your future (Jeremiah 29:11) more as dreams or intentions and less as a blueprint?

6. Review the Scriptures on page 88. How do these passages show more of God's fluid intentions than unchangeable blueprints?

> **"God has created you to be engaged in history and to be engaged in the creation of the future."**

7. What impact might this perspective have on what it means to you to be a Christian?

8. What do you need to do to best position yourself to partner with God to create the future?

> ✶ **"Every religion in the world prays. ... What makes us different is that when we pray, God hears, and our conversation and communion and relationship with God actually affects what God does in human history."**

9. How are prayers different when they're prayed to help create the future?

JOURNAL

This journaling opportunity is designed for group members to utilize at another time. They may choose to answer the question in the space provided or they may prefer to use the space and time to take a deep question or concern to God.

"Somebody is going to create the future. Why not us?"

What would it look like for you to begin moving forward more aggressively to partner with God to create God's preferred future—one that has your life as part of that future?

Acts 16:16 — Girl w/ Spirit who tells future.

- When we pray, God hears & our

YOU'RE UP

As you wrestle with your role in partnering with God to create the future, think about the following:

- Ask God to help you see the ways He's already given you permission to create.

- Reflect on the Scriptures and ask God to speak to you in response to what you have to offer the world—the good God has placed inside of you.

- Challenge perspectives that say the future is some sort of f xed inevitability. Explore the anxiety that comes with responsibility and ask God for the courage to embrace that responsibility.

- Enjoy the possibility that God's preferred future is better than the present that exists today.

GROUP DIRECTORY

NAME: _____
HOME PHONE: _____
MOBILE PHONE: _____
E-MAIL: _____
SOCIAL NETWORK (S): _____

NAME: _____
HOME PHONE: _____
MOBILE PHONE: _____
E-MAIL: _____
SOCIAL NETWORK (S): _____

NAME: _____
HOME PHONE: _____
MOBILE PHONE _____
E-MAIL: _____
SOCIAL NETWORK (S): _____

NAME: _____
HOME PHONE: _____
MOBILE PHONE: _____
E-MAIL: _____
SOCIAL NETWORK (S): _____

NAME: _____
HOME PHONE: _____
MOBILE PHONE: _____
E-MAIL: _____
SOCIAL NETWORK (S): _____

NAME: _____
HOME PHONE: _____
MOBILE PHONE: _____
E-MAIL: _____
SOCIAL NETWORK (S): _____

NAME: _____
HOME PHONE: _____
MOBILE PHONE: _____
E-MAIL: _____
SOCIAL NETWORK (S): _____

NAME: _____
HOME PHONE: _____
MOBILE PHONE: _____
E-MAIL: _____
SOCIAL NETWORK (S): _____

NAME: _____
HOME PHONE: _____
MOBILE PHONE: _____
E-MAIL: _____
SOCIAL NETWORK (S): _____

NAME: _____
HOME PHONE: _____
MOBILE PHONE: _____
E-MAIL: _____
SOCIAL NETWORK (S): _____

NAME: _____
HOME PHONE: _____
MOBILE PHONE: _____
E-MAIL: _____
SOCIAL NETWORK (S): _____

NAME: _____
HOME PHONE: _____
MOBILE PHONE: _____
E-MAIL: _____
SOCIAL NETWORK (S): _____